Sports and Activities

Let's Ice-Skate!

by Carol K. Lindeen

Consulting Editor: Gail Saunders-Smith, PhD

Consultant: Kymm Ballard, MA
Physical Education, Athletics, and Sports Medicine Consultant
North Carolina Department of Public Instruction

Capstone
press

Mankato, Minnesota

Pebble Plus is published by Capstone Press,
151 Good Counsel Drive, P.O. Box 669, Mankato, Minnesota 56002.
www.capstonepress.com

1 2 3 4 5 6 11 10 09 08 07 06

Library of Congress Cataloging-in-Publication Data
Lindeen, Carol K., 1976–
    Let's ice-skate! / by Carol K. Lindeen.
    p. cm.—(Pebble plus. Sports and activities)
    Includes bibliographical references and index.
    ISBN-13: 978-0-7368-5360-6 (hardcover)
    ISBN-10: 0-7368-5360-X (hardcover)
    1. Skating—Juvenile literature. I. Title. II. Series.
GV850.223.L55 2006
796.91—dc22   2005017940

Summary: Simple text and photographs present the skills, equipment, and safety concerns of ice-skating.

Editorial Credits
Heather Adamson, editor; Kia Adams, designer; Kelly Garvin, photo researcher

Photo Credits
Capstone Press/Karon Dubke, 15 (boy); TJ Thoraldson Digital Photography, cover, 1, 7, 9, 11, 17
Corbis/Don Mason, 19; Michael Prince, 15 (background); Tom Stewart, 21
Getty Images/Stone/Lori Adamski Peek, 5
Index Stock Imagery/Omni Photo Communications Inc., 13

Note to Parents and Teachers

The Sports and Activities set supports national physical education standards related
to recognizing movement forms and exhibiting a physically active lifestyle. This book
describes and illustrates ice-skating. The images support early readers in understanding
the text. The repetition of words and phrases helps early readers learn new words.
This book also introduces early readers to subject-specific vocabulary words, which are
defined in the Glossary section. Early readers may need assistance to read some words
and to use the Table of Contents, Glossary, Read More, Internet Sites, and Index sections
of the book.

Table of Contents

Ice-Skating

Glide and spin,

around the rink we go.

It's fun to ice-skate

with friends.

Ice-skaters hold hands.

They make a chain

and skate together.

Some ice-skaters skate

on one foot.

Sometimes they jump!

Ice-skaters skate forward
and backward.
They push their skates
to move fast or slow.

Ice rinks have smooth ice
made just for skating.
Some rinks are indoors.
Some are outdoors.

Skates

Ice skates fit like boots.

The metal blades help skaters

move on the ice.

Skating Safety

Ice is cold!

Ice-skaters wear thick socks.

They wear hats and mittens

to stay warm.

Ice-skating takes practice.

Coaches help new

skaters learn.

Having Fun

Let's slide and glide
over the cool ice.
Let's ice-skate!

Glossary

blades—long, thin strips of metal that are sharp on one edge

coach—a person who teaches or trains an athlete or a team

glide—to move or slide in a smooth, quiet way

rink—a large, flat sheet of ice for ice-skating; ice rinks can be indoors or outdoors.

spin—to twirl or turn around and around

Read More

Bray-Moffatt, Naia. *Ice Skating School.* New York: DK Publishing, 2004.

Eckart, Edana. *I Can Ice Skate.* Sports. New York: Children's Press, 2002.

Klingel, Cynthia. *Ice Skating.* Wonder Books. Chanhassen, Minn.: Child's World, 2003.

Internet Sites

FactHound offers a safe, fun way to find Internet sites related to this book. All of the sites on FactHound have been researched by our staff.

Here's how:

1. Visit *www.facthound.com*

2. Type in this special code **073685360X** for age-appropriate sites. Or enter a search word related to this book for a more general search.

3. Click on the **Fetch It** button.

FactHound will fetch the best sites for you!

Index

Word Count: 110
Grade: 1
Early-Intervention Level: 12